THE SOLO AGER ESTATE PLAN

TRUST AND ESTATE ESSENTIALS FOR SINGLE, CHILDLESS SENIORS

ANTHONY S. PARK

ISBN: 9798645698485

www.anthonyspark.com

Cover design by JD Smith Design

DEDICATION

For every Solo Ager who has entrusted me with their legacy

THANK YOU FOR YOUR FEEDBACK

Hearing directly from you, the reader, is the best way for me to make these books as useful as possible.

Please share how this book has helped you, or any suggestions for how I can make it better. You can email me at SoloAger@anthonyspark.com or call me at 212-401-2990.

Thanks in advance for your feedback.

Best,

Anthony S. Park

CONTENTS

INTRODUCTION

WHO THIS BOOK IS FOR

Most estate planning guides are written for starter families. Or, they're generic, trying to cover all possible generations and scenarios.

Not this one. This book is just for Solo Agers: single seniors without children or grandchildren.

I'm a practicing lawyer and professional executor in New York. So this book is definitely New York-centric. But most of the general concepts in here will help you, even if you're not from the Big Apple.

TAKEAWAYS

If I can leave you with three takeaways from this book, they'll be:

1. Your estate plan protects *you*. It's not just about what happens after you die.
2. Most default estate planning laws were not written with Solo Agers in mind. That's why you need a customized estate plan.
3. Yes, there are professionals to fill all the estate planning roles (trustee, executor, etc.) that you thought had to be friends or family.

BRIEF OUTLINE

We'll start in Chapters 1 and 2 by defining Solo Agers, and explaining why their estate plans need to be different.

Then in Chapters 3 through 5, we'll go deeper into the three biggest differences: how your estate plan protects you, choosing your heirs, and hiring a pro to manage your estate.

Lastly, in Chapters 6 and 7, I'll run down the checklist of documents in your estate plan and answer your most frequently asked questions.

I use many real-life examples from my decades as an attorney, executor, and trustee. Of course, I've changed names and details to protect privacy.

Let's get started.

CHAPTER 1

WHO ARE SOLO AGERS?

"Solo Agers" are single seniors without children or grandchildren. I'll go into more detail later, but first a note on the nickname for your demographic.

THE NAME "SOLO AGERS"

I struggled when deciding which nickname to use. Google says the three most common are: Elder Orphans, Solo Seniors, and Solo Agers.

I eliminated Elder Orphans because "orphans" is a bit of a downer (thanks, Oliver Twist). I was leaning toward Solo Seniors, but apparently "Senior" is politically incorrect lately. Who knew?

So I landed on Solo Agers by process of elimination. I hope you agree.

YOU'RE IN GOOD COMPANY

Solo Agers enjoy living alone because of their independence. You probably also enjoy more freedom than your friends who have more family ties.

More and more folks see it this way. Almost 12 million Americans age 65 and older live alone. That's nearly 25% of all people over 65.

For fun, here's a list of just a few famous Solo Agers:

- Sir Isaac Newton
- Leonardo DaVinci
- Ludwig van Beethoven
- Nikola Tesla
- Raymond Burr
- Luther Vandross
- Patrick Swayze
- Ralph Fiennes
- Bob Barker

Now back to the details on who Solo Agers are.

SINGLE

Solo Agers are single. Or widowed. Or divorced. Basically, anyone without a surviving spouse.

Why is this important? Because a surviving spouse comes with all sorts of estate planning rights and implications. Just a few examples:

- "Which spouse dies first" contingencies
- Spousal support trust needed
- Spousal right of election planning
- Estate tax exemption planning for surviving spouse
- Scramble to update your estate plan upon divorce

Singlehood means you don't have a "default" for many estate planning roles. Married folks usually name their spouse as executor, trustee, health care proxy, and heir. And state laws also assume a surviving spouse should fill those roles. In later chapters, I'll talk about why these defaults can be mistakes, anyway.

Important note: if you live alone, separated from a wife you never legally divorced, you are NOT single. I hate to break it to you, but you will have a surviving spouse (at least under New York law). You might be surprised how often this happens.

Example: Greg and Carrie were married for just a year in the 70s. They decided to split, and went on to live completely separate lives for the next 50 years. But they never got a formal divorce.

Greg wanted to leave his condo to his loving niece, Marcia. Marcia had cared for Greg through his achy final years. But when Greg died without a plan, the probate court ordered Marcia to find Greg's long-lost "wife," Carrie. Sadly, Carrie inherited Greg's condo and everything else he owned. Marcia received nothing.

Greg should've gotten a divorce, or a better estate plan.

65+ YEARS OLD

Solo Agers are over 65 years old, but this number isn't set in stone like the driving or voting age. It's about whether you've reached a stage of life with more certainty, and fewer variables. Some examples:

Career. You're working your final job or retired. So you can focus your estate plan on investments, required distributions, and retirement income. You aren't worried about 401k rollovers or vesting stock options from your new startup.

Family Tree. Your lineage is set. Yes, it's possible to keep siring kids (look at Hef). But odds are you're done, so you know for sure who your direct descendants are. This means your estate plan doesn't have to be as flexible, and we can prepare with more certainty.

Financial Structure. Once you reach a certain age, you tend to get comfortable with your bank and brokerage. So moving from Chase to Capital One, or from Vanguard to Schwab becomes less likely.

Compare that to folks who are early- or mid-career. They're constantly switching banks to get a few extra crumbs of interest. Or opening an account with that new brokerage because they have a fancy new app.

Here's one example of how estate planning is different if you have fixed financial accounts: Solo Agers can use tools such as beneficiary designations in their plans. Non-seniors change banks too often, so their beneficiary designations become a tangled mess.

Example: Igor is the kind of guy who learns from other people's mistakes. Like when his nephew Peter died at just 45 years old, survived by his wife Yvonne and their young kids.

Peter had a do-it-yourself will leaving everything to Yvonne and the kids. He even named them as beneficiaries on most of his accounts. Pretty good...

But Peter had many jobs during his career, so he had more 401k accounts than he could keep track of. One named his brother as beneficiary, and another his mom. The biggest problem was that Peter had some valuable stock options from a startup he joined way back. He forgot that he had named his girlfriend at the time (not Yvonne!) as beneficiary of that large account. That ex-girlfriend quietly collected the account for herself, and did not return Yvonne's calls.

Peter's estate mess inspired Igor to check his own estate plan. All of Igor's accounts are owned by his trust or name his trust as beneficiary. He's retired and has been with the same bank and brokerage for 15 years, with no plans to change. Whew! Igor's estate won't be a mess like Peter's.

CHILDLESS

Solo Agers are childless. Maybe you never had kids or grandkids. Or maybe you have kids, but they're estranged. Or they only call once in a blue moon when they need something.

Whichever version of "childless" applies to you, congratulations on your freedom! What do I mean? Well, most parents feel compelled to leave most of their wealth to their kids. It's liberating to watch my Solo Ager clients decide who will inherit their estate. Your choices are limitless! All to the one niece who's good to you? Sure! Favorite charity? You bet!

Example: Every week, friends Michael, Alan, and Jack pick up coffee and donuts and meet in the park to chat and catch up. They often compare notes about their estate plans.

Michael is a widower with three grown kids. His kids are great, but they have their own lives. Michael is much closer to his friends, like Alan and Jack. Michael would like to leave something to his pals, but he feels pressure to leave only to his family.

Alan is divorced with no children. He has a dozen nieces and nephews. But only one niece keeps in touch with Alan, and he knows she deserves a larger inheritance than the rest. But he can't shake the feeling that he's "supposed" to give them equal shares. And he doesn't want to upset his siblings. It's a bit stressful.

Jack never married, never had kids. He loves his adorable grandnieces and nephews, and he cherishes his friends. He also has a few causes he'd like to support. Jack doesn't feel any pressure or guilt about his choices, and can't wait to decide how to leave his legacy.

You can probably tell that Jack leaves these chats feeling better than his pals.

If you don't quite fit the definition of a Solo Ager, feel free to keep reading anyway. I hope you'll learn from chapters that *do* fit your life.

CHAPTER 2

WHY YOU NEED A DIFFERENT ESTATE PLAN

Over the years, I've noticed that Solo Ager estate planning wishes are very different from what happens under the default laws.

Every state has default laws that kick in if you don't have a customized estate plan. And those default laws pretty much assume you have a traditional nuclear family.

But Solo Agers have very different estate planning needs and preferences. Here are the three most common issues.

IF YOU BECOME VULNERABLE

Once you reach a certain age, you need to start planning for when you're more vulnerable. Right now, your independence is great. But you can't beat Father Time forever.

I'll talk about "vulnerable" in more detail in the next chapter. For now, just know that I mean things like coma, dementia, or gradual senility.

Nuclear family folks assume their spouse or adult kids will care for them. And in fact, even without an estate plan, most state default laws place the spouse or kids in charge. As a Solo Ager, you need to actively make other arrangements. Otherwise, the courts may assign a complete stranger as your guardian.

Whether you want a relative, a friend, or a trusted professional to be in charge, you need a customized plan for the event you become vulnerable.

NON-TRADITIONAL HEIRS

Default inheritance laws assume you want to leave your stuff to your closest living relatives. But many Solo Agers want to leave inheritance to relatives who sit on more distant branches of the family tree. Or, they want to leave parts of their estate to charitable causes.

Again, you need a customized estate plan to document your wishes. Plus, a solid plan will ensure your money goes to those intended, and not to creditors or the IRS.

NO ASSUMED EXECUTOR

Lastly, Solo Agers get to avoid the common mistake of naming a spouse or kid as their executor or trustee. Maybe because they feel free to hire a professional executor or trustee, and reap the many advantages that come with it.

CHAPTER 3

TO PROTECT YOU, NOT JUST YOUR HEIRS

MANY SOLO AGERS THINK: "ESTATE PLANNING ONLY helps my heirs after I'm dead. But once I'm dead, I really don't care. So why should I bother making a plan?"

Let me correct the main assumption, that "estate planning only helps my heirs after I'm dead." Not true! Your estate plan will actually protect *you*, during your life, as you age and grow more vulnerable.

WHAT DO YOU MEAN BY "VULNERABLE?"

Bluntly, we all break down as we age. Some of us will hold out longer than others, but eventually Father Time wins.

Maybe your body shuts down, as in a coma or vegetative state. So you're alive, but not awake to make your own health care decisions. And while you're out, your financial affairs may fall into disarray.

Or, perhaps you gradually slide downhill toward senility or

dementia. I agree, it's not easy to think about, but we've all seen it happen to our friends and loved ones.

And finally, even if you're physically ok and you've got all your marbles, you may simply become frail, less robust than you're used to. And unfortunately, bad guys love to prey on our weakened citizens and impose their will on them.

Example: Bruce is the last guy you'd worry about being "vulnerable."

He's a former track and field star, and remains very fit. After he retired from athletics, he went on to enjoy a long and successful business career.

When we first chatted about estate planning for his protection, Bruce scoffed. He has no family history of senility or dementia. And if he goes into a coma, he figures his survival odds are low, so who cares?

A few years later, Bruce has noticed some changes. He gets tired quicker. His stamina is a bit lower. Nothing major, but it *is* impacting his life.

That rude clerk at the supermarket keeps pushing his limits. Before, Bruce would have put him in his place. But nowadays, it's not worth his energy.

And pushy salesmen seem to be having more of their way with him. Bruce used to chew these guys up, but now they're wearing him down.

Yes, Bruce still has all his senses. But it wouldn't hurt to have an advocate in his estate plan. Just in case.

You may be thinking: "Sure, I think about those things, but the legal system will protect me, right?"

COURT-APPOINTED STRANGERS

What happens if you do nothing or have a poor estate plan? Yes, there are default state laws and courts. But I have yet to meet someone who's enjoyed going through "the system." The big problem is, the court will appoint strangers to control your life, your health, and your money.

How do you end up in the system? Sometimes a stranger thinks you're not all there. She can be a teller at your bank who thinks a transaction seems odd. Or a well-meaning social worker who thinks you should be evaluated, for your own good, of course.

Next, a doctor will examine you to decide if you're able to make your own decisions. Often, this is not your primary care physician, but a court-appointed doctor you've never met before. He will recommend to the court whether you need a court-appointed guardian to take over your health or financial decisions.

Lastly, the court will appoint your guardian. The judge may choose a relative, even if that cousin is the *last* person you'd ever want. Or, he may appoint an attorney who's a complete stranger. Either way, this person will have full legal authority over your medical and financial life.

Example: Joe might have the worst luck in the world with court-appointed strangers.

See, Joe was finally going to buy that dream car he'd always wanted. So he went to the bank to draw a large cashier's check. Over the years, Joe's bank had evolved from a neighborhood bank to one of those megabanks. The tellers used to all know him by name, but now the faces changed so fast, he didn't know a soul.

The unfamiliar teller was wary of a senior making such a large withdrawal. Joe tried to explain, but got frustrated and stormed out without his check.

Back home, Joe soon received an unexpected visitor. The bank had called Adult Protective Services, which sent a doctor to examine Joe. The strange doctor asked Joe a few questions through the door, before Joe demanded to be left alone.

Things quickly spun out of control. Joe began receiving letters and official court papers that he didn't understand. Before he knew what was happening, a judge made a ruling based on the doctor's "examination" that Joe was unfit to manage his own affairs.

The judge chose a court-appointed lawyer to be Joe's guardian. The guardian took over all of Joe's bank accounts. Every time Joe had a simple question, his "guardian" was billing an hourly rate!

Finally, Joe figured out how to ask the court to change guardians. Out of desperation to get away from the lawyer, Joe nominated a nephew he barely knew. The judge allowed it, but only after paying the lawyer's hefty fees from Joe's accounts.

Finally, Joe asked his nephew for permission to buy his dream sports car with his own money. The unfamiliar nephew said no.

Please remember this horrible example. In the next section, we'll visit an alternate reality where Joe had an estate plan and avoided all this.

What's wrong with having strangers in charge of your life? One, a stranger doesn't know you or your quirks, sense of humor, or preferences, yet will make all your big life decisions? Two, the system is like any other bureaucracy: many of the players are indifferent, incompetent, or both! And lastly, even within the legal system, there's plenty of financial rip-offs.

HOW YOUR ESTATE PLAN PROTECTS YOU

Your plan isn't just a stack of papers. It's also bringing together your trusted team, including your primary care physician (yes, they still exist), your lawyer, your CPA and your financial advisor.

Your financial advisor and lawyer will help you avoid raising red flags at your banks. Your doctor and lawyer will shield you from false diagnoses by a random court-appointed physician. And if you actually are in decline and need help, a court-appointed stranger won't be in charge. It'll be your pre-selected trustee and lawyer—people you trust who know you and your preferences. Someone like me will keep your finances in order, make sure your bills are paid, etc.

> *Example*: Let's revisit Joe's story, and how much more awesome his life would be with a solid estate plan and team.
>
> Instead of going to the bank himself, Joe would ask his financial advisor to arrange the check. Or, after going to the bank himself, he could ask his lawyer to place a stern call to the bank to set things straight.
>
> Suppose it got so far as a strange, court-appointed doctor appearing at his door. Joe would tell the unannounced visitor, "Call my lawyer." Joe's lawyer would make sure a medical evaluation included an opinion from Joe's primary care physician.

If the process went before a judge, Joe would have his own lawyer explaining every step. And if the Judge ruled that Joe needed a guardian? Then Joe's pre-selected trustee of his trust would step in, and not some stranger.

Big difference, huh? Joe has a team and advocates on his side the whole way. No court-appointed strangers controlling him or his money.

And, let's not forget, Joe gets his dream sports car.

As a bonus, a solid estate plan is also a deterrent. Bad actors are opportunistic; they want low-hanging fruit. But once they see your team and estate plan, they'll know it'll be hard for them to take advantage or score a few dollars. So they'll move on, and you'll avoid the headache of entering the system.

CHAPTER 4

TO SECURE YOUR LEGACY

LEGACY IS IMPORTANT TO ALL OF US, AND ESPECIALLY for Solo Agers. You're uniquely free to choose your heirs as you see fit, without feeling pressure from societal norms. You're not "supposed to" leave your money to your distant family. At least not with the same level of expectation as with a spouse or children.

So, how do you make the most of this freedom to choose your own legacy?

FREE FROM DEFAULT LAWS

First, learn who would inherit from you under default laws. By default, inheritance goes to your blood relatives—and rarely in the proportions that match your wishes.

Most Solo Agers are single with no children. Their parents are usually predeceased. So, in most states, your heirs will be some combination of your siblings, nieces and nephews.

But the default laws can also result in some very skewed outcomes.

Example: Robert thought he knew his family tree, but he didn't. His mistake kind of ruined his legacy.

Robert was single with no kids. His parents had predeceased, and he was an only child. But he was close with his two aunts, and eight cousins from his dad's side.

Unfortunately, Robert got sick and had to start thinking about his final affairs. He thought the default law would divide his assets equally among his aunts and cousins. Not exactly how he'd want it, but close enough. So he decided to save a few bucks, and skip a lawyer and estate plan.

After Robert died, his favorite aunt, Rose, tried to probate his estate. That's when Edmund—an estranged cousin Robert didn't realize he had on his mom's side—entered the picture.

So what happened? The judge ruled to divide Robert's estate into two halves: one for relatives on his mother's side, and the other for relatives on his father's. Edmund, a total stranger, ended up inheriting one half (!) of Robert's estate because he was the only surviving relative on the mother's side. Meanwhile, each of the 10 close relatives on his father's side received only one tenth of the other half of Robert's estate.

You are not obligated to leave your family equal shares or to include everyone. Feel free to pick and choose based on whom you have a good relationship with, or whatever your reason. But you need an estate plan to opt out of those default laws and make sure your estate goes to your chosen heirs.

YOUR LEGACY OF GIVING

If they don't have a close or favorite family member, Solo Agers often create a legacy by giving to a cause. Here are two tips on how to leave your charitable legacy.

First, make your gift to a charitable *cause*, not to a specific charity. Why? Organizations, even charities, change and evolve over time. You probably know a few charities that once completely aligned with your values. But over time, the percentage of money that actually goes to supporting the charitable work has fallen. Or executive compensation has crept up.

Example: Do you support charity organizations whose CEO earns over $1 million per year?

Here are a few well-known charities whose CEO compensation has crept over that mark in recent years:

• American Heart Association - $2.3 million

• Wildlife Conservation Society - $1.6 million

• New York Blood Center - $1.5 million

• Visiting Nurse Service of New York - $1.4 million

• St. Jude Children's Research Hospital - $1.2 million

• Boy Scouts of America - $1.2 million

• New York Public Radio - $1.1 million

• United Way Worldwide - $1 million

Or, say your favorite charity remains a lean, well-oiled machine. But what if its underlying mission changes? Charities rarely explicitly alter their mission, but they may change in ways inconsistent with your cause.

Example: Say you support a Christian charity that builds local community churches. How would you feel if they changed their focus to overseas missionary work instead?

Or, say your favorite education charity helps public schools. What if that charity suddenly gets more political? Such as fighting for teachers unions or charter schools?

Second, leave a lasting legacy that gives every year, not a single lump-sum inheritance. You may be thinking that a large one-time gift upon your death is more bang for your buck. But I'm telling you, that big one-time gift, and your legacy, will be forgotten within a year. I see it all the time.

A great example of this is leaving a one-time gift to your alma mater, versus an annual scholarship:

Example: Barry and George both love their alma maters and want to leave them a legacy. Neither is so wealthy that he can leave a building (or heck, even get his name on a bench plaque). But they'd both like to be remembered.

> Barry decides to make a "big splash" by leaving a lump sum upon his death. It works...kind of. Barry's trustee receives a nice letter directly from the university president. And Barry's name is listed prominently in that year's alumni newsletter.
>
> But just a year or two later, no one at his alma mater even remembers Barry. They've moved on.
>
> George decides to make his gift last. Instead of a single large gift, he instructs his trustee to invest that money. From the trust income, the trustee awards annual scholarship grants in George's name.
>
> Every year, young students and their families take a moment to acknowledge and appreciate George's generous gift. And George's legacy will last for many years to come.

You can use both these tips—give to a cause, not an organization, and leave long-lasting gifts over time—by giving in trust, our next topic.

ALWAYS LEAVE GIFTS IN TRUST FUNDS

How do you make sure your legacy actually goes the way you want? You've spent time and energy thinking carefully about who gets what. Won't you feel frustrated if it all turns out different? You can ensure control of your legacy by always using trusts.

When most of us imagine our estate plan, we think of direct

gifts. "I leave my Chase bank account to my nephew Carlton," for example. And upon your death, Carlton gets the cash in the Chase account—it's his.

Instead, your estate plan should say, "I leave my Chase bank account in continuing trust for my nephew Carlton." Then, upon your death, your trustee holds and invests your Chase account on Carlton's behalf.

Why? If you've decided to leave your legacy as a direct gift to a friend or family member, you want them to actually receive it, right? But in today's world, you probably know folks who have gone through any number of tough situations:

1. Divorce
2. Debt
3. Problems with the IRS
4. Trouble with scammers

If any of these common situations apply to your heir, then they may never get their inheritance. Instead, your hard-earned legacy may go to: an ex-spouse, a creditor, the IRS, or a Nigerian scammer.

The good news is, you can easily avoid this. To make sure your favorite niece actually receives your money, leave her inheritance in a trust. A properly set-up trust in your estate plan is bulletproof asset protection for your heirs.

And it's an amazing gift your heir could never give herself. Why? The way laws work, it's very hard to protect your assets *once you've received them.* The next best thing is some crazy offshore accounts (like in the movies). But those are super expensive and actually won't work as well as an inheritance by trust. Because by receiving their inheritance in trust, your heirs have never actually "owned" your money.

Example: All of Charlie's bad luck got erased by one stroke of good luck.

Charlie married poorly and got divorced. His ex was constantly after him for more money. Then his business got crushed by the recent recession. Creditors called him all the time and he began considering bankruptcy. He was also in an IRS audit. Enough said.

Thankfully, Charlie finally had some good luck. His uncle died and left Charlie an inheritance. But that's not the "good luck." The good luck was that Charlie's uncle was smart enough to leave the inheritance in trust.

Now Charlie's inheritance is protected. That money was never under Charlie's control. So Charlie's ex can't get to it—not even with a divorce court order. Neither can his business creditors or the IRS, even in bankruptcy.

All the while, the trustee can pay for Charlie's rent and other living expenses. And Charlie knows that once his bad luck runs out, his full inheritance will still be there for him in trust.

As we talked about earlier in this chapter, you should also leave your charitable gifts in trust. Your charitable trust will make sure your legacy goes to a cause you care about. And it will stretch your memory over years, not just a one-time flash in the pan.

CHAPTER 5

TO CHOOSE THE RIGHT MANAGER FOR YOUR LEGACY

WHAT'S THE POINT OF SPENDING YOUR TIME AND mental energy on your estate plan if nothing goes as planned when you die?

Even the best estate plan is not a robot. There's no artificial intelligence (yet) that will trigger and automatically carry out your wishes when you die. The estate process still has plenty of human elements. Your trustee, executor, and others must manage and actually execute your plan.

Let's talk about some common mistakes for choosing your executor or trustee. And when it makes sense to hire a professional.

AVOID THESE COMMON BAD CHOICES

I call the first big mistake the "Best Man" fallacy. This is when you choose your executor or trustee like you would the best man at your wedding. You go with your best friend or your closest relative. While that may be the best person for a great wedding toast, your ideal executor or trustee should understand the law, taxes, and personal finance. Not just have a great story to share from your "glory days."

Even if your "best man" candidate has the financial skills, he may not have time to take on this important role for you. Being an executor is very time-intensive for several months after your death. Your family and friends may have their own busy careers, or may simply need time to mourn your passing.

Also, consider a person's age. Bluntly, your executor needs to outlive you. And your trustees not only need to outlive you, but ideally have a few prime decades left in them. So they're around long enough to protect the money left to your heirs or favorite charitable causes.

Lastly, a common mistake is treating the role of executor or trustee as a "gift." Yes, each role comes with paid compensation (more on that later in Chapter 7). But it's a job, and sometimes a very stressful and risky job—not a gift.

> *Example*: Who did Tony choose as his trustee: his brother, his best friend, or his closest friend living nearby? Answer: none of the above.
>
> Tony and his brother Joe were on speaking terms, but they fought about almost everything. So even though Joe was his closest relative, Tony immediately vetoed him.

Jack had been Tony's best friend for over 60 years. Tony trusted Jack completely. And Jack was a savvy businessman with legal, accounting, and tax knowledge. But Jack lived in North Carolina, not Tony's home state of New York. And Tony could not ask him to keep flying back and forth to carry out the in-person duties of a trustee.

Nat was Tony's next-closest friend, a pal of over 40 years. And he lived right here in New York. Nat could also use a few extra bucks, so Tony thought the trustee's fee would help him out. But then Tony remembered that Nat had a few health issues that would make running around the city tough.

The final straw was when Tony decided that most of his estate would go into a trust. The trust would pay his brother Joe during his life. And when Joe died, the trust would continue for his grandkids. Joe, Jack, and Nat were all in their late 60s. So they'd probably be quite old, or even deceased, and unable to manage the trust till the end.

So what did Tony decide? He hired me as his professional trustee. And he left an extra cash gift to help his pal Nat, instead of making Nat a trustee.

"I DON'T HAVE ANYONE TO BE MY EXECUTOR"

This is the most common worry I see among Solo Agers. I'd

like to ease your concerns by correcting two mistaken assumptions (1) your executor or trustee does not need to be a relative; and (2) yes, you can outsource it.

First, most people mistakenly believe their executor or trustee must be a close relative or trusted friend. Not only is this not necessarily true, it's often actually a bad choice.

Your executor or trustee does not have to be a relative. So you don't have to choose that estranged grandnephew or distant cousin you barely speak with.

It doesn't have to be someone you "trust." Of course, you shouldn't choose someone you know to be dishonest. But on the flip side, you don't need someone who knows your deepest secrets. There's a wide middle ground. And you're often better off with someone who will manage your final affairs professionally, but dispassionately.

> *Example*: Kristy made her best friend, Tina, a lawyer, her executor. What could go wrong?
>
> Kristy's passing was more emotionally draining on Tina than she expected. Cleaning out Kristy's apartment could have been done in a few days. But Tina lingered on anything that triggered fond memories. So the cleanout took weeks, instead.
>
> Then Kristy's estranged nephews came sniffing around for their inheritance. Where were they when Kristy was sick, and eventually dying? They didn't even make it to the funeral!

Tina was outraged, and it affected her decision-making. She dragged the nephews into an unnecessary court battle.

Probably not what Kristy imagined when she chose Tina as executor.

Second, if you can't think of a good candidate within your circle, you can hire a pro. If you didn't realize this is an option, don't feel bad. Most people don't know.

In past generations, only the uber-wealthy hired their banks or law firms as their executors and trustees. But lately, individual attorneys and smaller trust companies offer this service to everyday folks like me and you.

PROS OF HIRING A PRO

Does hiring a professional executor or trustee sound appealing to you? Probably. It's attractive for many Solo Agers. Here are my three biggest "pros" for hiring a professional. Please remember that I am a professional executor and trustee, so I'm probably biased.

First, professional executors and trustees are, well, *professionals*. We run many estates and trusts. We have the software and the relationships with courts and bankers. We have backgrounds and degrees in law, accounting, and business. Compare that with your distant cousin Larry, who may be involved with his first-ever estate. And he had to Google, "What is a trust?"

Second, you can find your pro from any generation. Your circle of friends is probably in your age group. As we discussed before, your executor needs to outlive you, and your trustee needs to be around even longer.

When searching for your pro, you want to find that sweet spot. Where he's young enough to outlast you, but not so young you can see the wet behind his ears. Older than 50, he may not outlast your trust. Younger than 35, he may lack seasoning and life experience.

And lastly, working with a pro doesn't cost you extra. When you name a professional executor or trustee in your estate plan, you don't pay a dime then. Why? Because he hasn't begun working as your executor/trustee yet. That happens later, when you pass.

When the time comes, your professional executor or trustee will be paid a fee set by state law. Your estate gets charged the same amount, whether you choose an experienced, professional attorney, or your couch-surfing, unemployed grandnephew. Which do you think is a better bang for your buck?

Example: Ronaldo needed a professional executor, but he was nervous about how much it would cost. He was pleasantly surprised when he learned the actual price.

Ronaldo's plan was to sell his apartment and leave the money in trust for his grandniece in Seattle. But who would manage his estate and trust? His best friend, Rudy, couldn't do it. He was around the same age and lived in Virginia.

When a friend referred me to Ronaldo as a professional trustee, Ronaldo was thrilled! He had no idea such a thing existed. But he was nervous that a "fancy lawyer-trustee" would cost him an arm and a leg.

He was relieved to learn there was no additional charge for naming me as his trustee. See, while Ronaldo was still alive, he managed his own trust alone. I was just a backup name on his estate plan papers.

Over the years, we chatted every few months to stay in touch. When Ronaldo passed, I was "activated" as his trustee.

I called Rudy, who handled the funeral and all family matters. And I set to work on Ronaldo's estate and trust. Only then did I earn any fees, a percentage set by state law, paid from trust.

I'm honored to continue managing Ronaldo's trust and legacy for his grateful grandniece.

This is only a brief overview of the pros of hiring a professional executor. To learn more, read my other book, *How to Hire an Executor*.

CHAPTER 6

ESTATE PLAN CHECKLIST FOR SOLO AGERS

THIS IS THE NITTY-GRITTY CHAPTER WHERE I DETAIL the exact documents you need in your estate plan:

1. Revocable living trust
2. Backup will
3. Advance directives

Remember, these documents are just a pile of paper. Your estate plan is really all your decisions and wishes that go into making these documents, plus your team that protects you and your wishes.

I also explain why I discourage you from using a power of attorney.

REVOCABLE LIVING TRUST

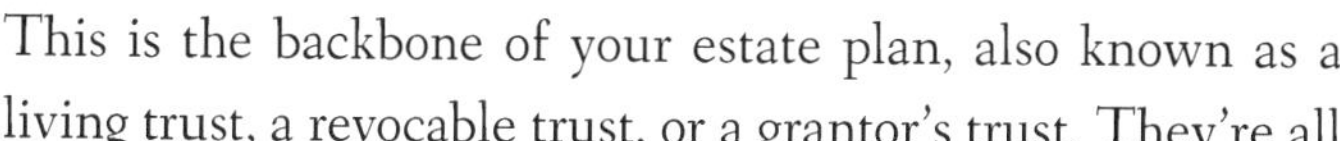

This is the backbone of your estate plan, also known as a living trust, a revocable trust, or a grantor's trust. They're all essentially the same thing. Not to be confused with a "living will," which is a health care document I'll discuss below. (Who comes up with these names? It's like they're trying to confuse us! Anyway...)

What exactly is your revocable living trust?

One way to think of your trust is a will-plus. Your trust does everything you'd probably expect from your will. It says who gets what and who's in charge after you die. But your trust is a "will-plus" because a will only works or kicks in after you're dead.

Your trust does all that, *and* protects you when you're alive. What happens if you fall into a coma or begin suffering from dementia? Your chosen trustee, not a court-appointed stranger, will make sure your finances continue running smoothly.

And, so long as you're alive and well, you're 100% in charge of your own trust. Your trustee only steps in to help if the court system deems you unable to manage your own affairs, or if you die.

Example: Bobby likes the idea of a trust to protect him, but hates the idea of giving up control or independence. Well, he's in luck...

Bobby loves his independence. The only thing worse than losing that, would be losing it to some court-appointed stranger. So he loves the idea of a trust as insurance against that situation.

But what about while Bobby is healthy and fine? Will his trustee meddle in his everyday life?

Nope. Here's how Bobby's trust works. First, he moves his accounts from his name to "The Bobby Revocable Trust." All that takes is filling out some bank and brokerage forms. Very easy.

Then, it's all business as usual for Bobby. Only he has access to his accounts.

But if something goes bad? If Bobby gets into an accident and is in a coma, or a court rules he's incompetent? *That's* when his trustee steps in. Bobby's trustee will make sure to pay his bills and manage his finances. And the trustee is someone Bobby knows and chose, not a random stranger.

Bobby gets his independence and his "insurance." Best of both worlds.

Your revocable living trust makes it very easy to leave inheritance in trust rather than direct gifts (as discussed in Chapter 4). You already have the trust structure and trustee in place. They simply carry on after your death for your heirs or charitable causes.

Lastly, you can sign your trust with zero in-person contact. A trust only needs to be notarized, which you can do by video chat and mail or FedEx. This feature is a big deal in our post-coronavirus world. And it also means updates to your trust are easier and less expensive.

BACKUP WILL

You'll need a will to back up your trust. You may be asking, "If I already have this great revocable living trust, why do I need a backup will?" Two reasons.

First, for any assets not in the trust. Your trust only works on assets and accounts that you've moved into the trust.

You may decide you want to keep your day-to-day checking account in your name rather than your trust's. Or, one financial institution may have too many bureaucratic rules for switching your account into your trust. Whatever the reason, your will is there to cover any assets not in your trust.

Second, you'll want to name in your will an executor who has legal authority for other things. Sure, your trustee can handle all your assets. But for legal issues, such as suing a hospital for your wrongful death, you'll need an executor named in your will.

Your will can be super simple. Here's the gist of what it should say: "For anything I didn't put into my trust, put it in my trust upon my death." Just remember, the probate court process for wills is brutal (to learn more about this, see my other book, *How Probate Works*). So we want to minimize the amount of assets outside of your trust. Your will is just backup to make sure all assets eventually get moved into the trust.

ADVANCE DIRECTIVES

These are the documents where you express your end-of-life and funeral wishes, and decide who will carry out those wishes. The three most common are your living will, health care proxy, and funeral directions.

Your living will is your instruction to withhold life-extending treatments if you are terminally ill or comatose with no hope of recovery. The list of treatments may include:

- CPR
- Mechanical respiration
- Feeding tube
- Intravenous feeding
- Blood transfusion
- Dialysis
- Antibiotics

Your health care proxy names the person you choose (your health care agent) to carry out the wishes in your living will.

Your funeral directions list your wishes for your remains and funeral, and name the person who will carry out your wishes. For your remains, specify whether you prefer burial or cremation. And express your religious or other preference for your funeral.

NO POWER OF ATTORNEY

You may have noticed that I haven't mentioned a power of attorney. I'm aware that many planners include them, but I discourage using general powers of attorney because they're overpowered and are too easy to abuse.

Example: The most famous, and saddest, example of power of attorney abuse is the story of Brooke Astor.

Brooke Astor married into the wealthy Astor family. She became known as the "First Lady of Philanthropy." She was famous for her dedicated support of the New York Public Library, the Metropolitan Museum of Art, and more.

As she aged and grew vulnerable, her son used a power of attorney to take over. He used it to steal tens of millions from her, and left her to spend her final years living in squalor.

A solid revocable living trust is the better version of a power of attorney, anyway.

CHAPTER 7

SOLO AGER ESTATE PLAN FAQS

We've covered a lot, so you probably have questions. I've got you covered. Here are answers to your most common questions.

WHEN SHOULD YOU START YOUR ESTATE PLAN?

Yesterday. Now. ASAP.

You may be thinking, "I don't need to worry about estate planning yet. I feel great, I'm strong and I'm sharp." But that's exactly why you should make your estate plan now, before any decline.

Think about it. If there's any doubt about whether you were competent enough to sign your plan, a judge is more likely to uphold a plan you made years ago. Why? Because that's when you were full of vim and vigor. Versus a plan you made just a few weeks or months before a doctor concludes you lack competence.

It's also important to create a long paper trail, a history of your wishes. A longer, more consistent history will make it much harder for you to get screwed by the system.

Example: If you're the judge, which estate plan would you uphold?

Lex made his estate plan a few months before he died at 75 years old. He was also on several medications that may have blurred his thinking.

Earl made his first estate plan over 10 years ago. Over the years, he made updates here and there, but no major changes. At 75 years old, right before he died, Earl made a final update that was consistent with all his other versions. He was on the same medications as Lex.

Without even knowing who inherited under their estate plans, which sounds more solid? How would you rule?

That's why you need to start now.

WHAT ARE THE STEPS IN THE ESTATE PLANNING PROCESS?

With a good lawyer, creating your estate plan will be easier than you think.

The whole process usually spans just a few weeks. And in a

rush situation, we can get it done within a week or so. But remember, a long consistent history is better than any rush job (see above).

Here are the four steps for my estate planning process. Most lawyers use a similar process.

1. **The first meeting**. We'll schedule a brief chat by phone to get to know each other. You'll already be familiar with my expertise based on my books, podcasts, or having been referred to me. You'll arrange payment to get started. (How much? More on fees, below.)
2. **Design meeting**. This is the meat and potatoes. I'll walk you through the custom design of your Solo Ager plan. We'll review how it protects you, choose who inherits, and decide who will fill each important role.
3. **Final confirmations**. After the design meeting, we'll process and summarize all your major decisions. I like to give you a few days to sleep on these big choices. Then I'll get back to you and confirm all the details before we finalize your plan.
4. **Signing**. Finally, the big day! You'll sign your estate plan. We can do this remotely if you have access to any video chat service.

HOW MUCH SHOULD ESTATE PLANNING COST?

You're probably wondering how much a great estate attorney will cost you. There's no universal answer, but I can narrow it down to some ballpark figures for you.

According to AARP, the nationwide average attorney fee for a revocable living trust ranges from $1,100 to 1,500.

As I'm sure you know, everything in major cities costs more, including attorneys. In New York City, for example, the average cost ranges from $2,000 to $5,000. Many lawyers can be flexible with their fees.

For example, I offer a reduced fee for any client who's read this book! So make sure to mention you read this when you call!

Finally, I caution you to stay away from do-it-yourself forms or bargain basement lawyers. As a probate lawyer, I see first-hand all the problems these create when you die.

If you want your plan to actually work the way intended, don't skimp. As the saying goes, you get what you pay for.

CHAPTER 8

NEXT STEPS

That's it!

I'd love to hear your thoughts and experiences. Email me at SoloAger@anthonyspark.com with any questions of feedback.

Thank you for reading.

IF YOU LIKED THIS BOOK...

Thanks for reading. If you enjoyed this book, I'd appreciate a short review. Please consider leaving your honest review on Amazon or your favorite store.

And join my email list for new book announcements: https://anthonyspark.com/join

ABOUT THE AUTHOR

Anthony is a New York executor, attorney, and entrepreneur. Anthony's cases have been featured in many places, including the *Wall Street Journal*, *New York Times*, CNBC, and *MarketWatch*.

Anthony also hosts the popular podcast *Simple Money Wins* (available on YouTube, iTunes, and anthonys-park.com).

ALSO BY ANTHONY S. PARK

How to Buy Your Perfect First Home: What Every First-Time Homebuyer Needs to Know

How Probate Works: A Guide for Executors, Heirs, and Families 

How to Hire an Executor: For Your Loved One's Estate or Your Will 

How to Get Promoted: Simple Steps to Better Title and Higher Pay

How to Invest for Retirement: A Simple Path to Retiring Rich, Independent, and Free

ular contact with the people I met in Spain, the logistics of distance keeps us from that. And yet the people I met remain in my heart; I suspect they will be there forever. These people moved me with their personal stories of triumph and tribulation, and I believe those I met were moved by intimate stories I shared with them. I sense there was purpose for each encounter, though I may not know fully of this until sometime in the future, if ever.

Still I trust this is so.

My fascination with such connections is equally about their uniqueness and about how they were enabled by the environment. The Camino creates an opportunity to trust people and my sense of the goodness of God seems to reward such an attitude. This unusual dirt trail presents an open society of introspective individuals who accept their own failings and brokenness, and try not to judge others for the same. The experience is an ideal of what humans can be when stripped of pretense and pressure. It is this trusted and trusting nature that paved the way for me to connect meaningfully. Among my failings is a quickness to judge and criticize, though for a month I managed to rise above my sometimes trivial nature. The Camino stage helped me set aside these traits suggesting I can find a means to accomplish the same elsewhere; to be a better person; to bring about the changes within which I need.

The simple time away from worldly accomplishments and material possessions worked a kind of magic in my imagination and with my heart. Although it took a few days to become accustomed to the lifestyle, its simplicity

Solo Agers need are different from "default" laws – assuming nuclear family. p9

—

You ~~will~~ may? become VULNERABLE p11

—

If you don't choose an agent – judge will appoint guardian – after "stranger intervention." p13

—

P32: TRUST, OVER TIME, HIRE PROFESS. TRUSTEE.

—

P34 TRUSTEES ARE PAID SAME FEE SET BY STATE, WHETHER PRO OR FAMILY, AFTER YOU PASS

—

P38 REVOKABLE LIVING TRUST NO POA

—

P40 WILL PROBATE SUCKS

WILL: ANYTHING NOT IN TRUST – PUT IT IN THE TRUST!

Made in the USA
Middletown, DE
03 February 2024